Simply for You™

A Collection of Love Poems

By Joseph Green-Bishop

www.simplyforyou.us

Published by
Bujo Publishing
3013 Manor Green Blvd.
Euless, TX 76039
joegreenbishop@aol.com
www.simplyforyou.us

Design by
Concepts Unlimited
www.ConceptsUnlimitedInc.com
303-449-2907

ISBN: 978-0-615-52374-3   (pbk)

12   13   14   15   16   0 9 8 7 6 5 4 3 2 1

Dedication

This book is dedicated to my wife, Trudi; my mother, Dorothy;
my sister, Gwennie; and my late sister, Denise.

It is also dedicated to all of those who have ever searched for love,
for tenderness and for joy.

Joseph Green-Bishop
Dallas, Texas

Table of Contents

"*I* had often thought I would not see you again, and I began to tremble like dust in the wind."

The Warmth of May

I pledge to you my soul this night,
and give you my heart with a fawn's delight.

I had often thought I would not see you again,
and I began to tremble like dust in the wind.

I look to the window and stare through the pane,
a bird soars skyward. I imagine for us the same.

I remove my shoes to walk through the snow,
my feet grow not cold, I am in love you well know.

I journey to the river,
whose waters speak of a new day.

When we shall be together,
to share the warmth of May.

"All of the things precious in life that I can think to give, I will give to you, I will give to you."

Simply for You

All of the things lovely in life that I can think to do
I will do for you,
I will do for you.

All of the things precious in life that I can think to give
I will give to you,
I will give to you.

All of the secrets buried deep in my soul, heretofore untold
I will tell to you,
I will tell to you.

All of the stories laid deep in your heart longing to be turned
I will turn for you,
I will turn for you.

All of the places on this earth and beyond that you long to see
I will see with you,
I will see with you.

All of the love in your soul burning to be touched
I will touch for you,
I will touch for you.

"It will not be long before the harvest time, and the wheat seeds begin to grow."

The Morning Cold

You need not fear me in the morning cold.
I shall cover you with woolens,
I shall feed your soul.

You need not go thirsty when the springs run dry.
I will bring you mountain water,
and draw raindrops from the sky.

You need not fear the stillness when the earth seems not to turn.
I will build a house near the ocean,
and urge the sun to burn.

You need not feel desperation when the foliage seems not to glow.
It will not be long before the harvest time,
and the wheat seeds begin to grow.

You need only to love me in the morning cold.
Simply cover me with woolens,
simply feed my soul.

"There was so much I did not understand, yet I thought I knew how to be a man."

Though Incomplete

And yes my life was incomplete though I had
planned so well, so sure, so neat.

Each day as I did sit to take my rest,
the raven called with anger and deceit.

While the melodies played softly through the air,
I grasped my chance, my moment, my dare.

During the nights when I was tired and cold,
it was love I needed, I was told.

There was so much I did not understand,
yet I thought I knew how to be a man.

The more simple things had eluded me,
not unlike a twig beside a twisted tree.

Then I learned that to a woman I must give,
and thus I found what it really meant to live.

"There is little sense in rushing this love, it may break or bend, my lover friend."

My Lover Friend

For now we will be friends, not lovers.
That will come later, perhaps in the fall.
My lover friend.

For now I will search for me, and you will seek you,
and we can exchange notes, fears, all.
My lover friend.

There is a truer light between the blue and clear.
Most never find it, know it. It is seldom near.
My lover friend.

There is little sense in rushing this love,
it may break or bend.
My lover friend.

"I live on the edge of the world it seems, and rarely do I look beyond the side."

Believing in You

I know that I could believe in you,
like I believed in the sunrise when I was small.
I know that I could share my life with you,
and make you happy, giving you my all and all.

I feel as though I have known you for years,
through the showers and the heavy rains.
I saw your face once when I was searching,
I knew your pause but not your name.

I live on the edge of the world it seems,
and rarely do I look beyond the side.
There are a few things I really do need,
and even fewer who I do in confide.

I would keep your secrets and wait
until you came home.
We would know days without clouds.
Our hearts would never roam.

I know that I could believe in you,
like I believed in the sunrise when I was small.
I know that I could share my life with you,
and make you happy, giving you my all and all.

"In the dawn she is most earnest, healing, alive and endearing the mist."

Dancer's Delight

It has not been without its pain,
this journey, this forward walk.
It has not been without frustration,
this climb of mountain's sides.
Dancer's Delight

It has been laced with glory, too.
Steps sweetly touching steps,
grace smiling tenderly on grace.
Dancer's Delight

In the dawn she is most earnest,
healing, alive and endearing the mist.
In the twilight she is even stronger,
and while she is adored she is missed.
Dancer's Delight.

Her reward is beyond the stars,
her treat beneath the last ocean.
The final warming abounds her presence,
making the ballerina's flight complete.
Dancer's Delight.

Never an ending, only beginnings,
in her life and in her solitude.
Her spirit bound by the wind and truth.
Dancer's Delight.

There are only lilacs, sweet melodies,
legions of joy, silent and enduring.
Dancer's Delight.

"And ten thousand miles away I felt the warmth of your heart as you made me happy beyond happiness."

All Is Same

It is morning still, and the sleep is falling from your eyes.
The brown locks now laced with gray, evermore lovely.

Your life is like the sweetest of garden flowers,
just as when we were younger.

It was then that I knew your love was special,
there was something glorious and wonderful,
And now all is same.

One night I watched your face and looked into
your tender soul, before the oceans came between us.

And ten thousand miles away I felt the warmth
of your heart, as you made me happy beyond happiness.

You are my music during the silence,
making the lilies bloom
and the hillsides lush with green,
And now all is same.

"At the morning table you won me forever, lacing my life with your sun."

The Morning Table

At the morning table you captured my heart
and left me undone.

At the morning table you won me forever,
lacing my life with your sun.

At the morning table you romanced me
with your style and with your touch.

At the morning table the world stopped for a second,
for love, for much.

At the morning table your flowers still sit and wait.

At the morning table you blushed my soul and stroked my fate.

At the morning table time means little anymore.

At the morning table I wait your presence at my door.

At the morning table I sit, and stare where you once sat.

"Let me be your friend, drawing on your heart and pulling your soul nearer."

Complement My Life

Complement my life and help me see through this
thick forest of living.

Help me in this world
and let me grow to love you easy, so easy.

Be my source of comfort and let me come to you,
when no one else will hear my cry.

Let me be your friend, drawing on your heart
and pulling your soul nearer.

I would give you sunshine and more than all of me
each day that we live.

Never would I leave you nor retreat from loving you sweetly.

Ever would I need you and love you so completely.

"Large brown eyes and tiny black plaits, with warmth she comes to me."

Twilight and Morning Bright

Twilight and morning bright and Sunday afternoons,
sparkling streams and prescient thoughts and
midnight walks in June.

Fragrant balm and delicate cloth and waking half past noon,
lovely songs and bubble baths and mother like gentleness soon.

Large brown eyes and tiny black plaits, with warmth
she comes to me, like bow to the arrow,
as light to the blind, she helps to make me free.

Three short years and wayward tears, the time goes patiently.
Rush on the day when I kiss her hand and then weep tenderly.

"The cords of my heart sweetly play your song, the melody reaches for you, and winter is gone."

Moments

I would wait a thousand moments or more,
to spend a single one with you.

I would struggle through thousands of empty nights,
just to hold you for one delight.

Oh, how I would love to strengthen your soul,
to warm you while we are young and journey old.

The cords of my heart sweetly play your song,
the melody reaches for you, and winter is gone.

The moments of life are precious and few,
and if I can, I will share them with you.

"Do not be afraid to dream, always longing for the best while leaving the unrest."

Dream

Do not be afraid to dream as you dare to fly,
casting your fate to the sky.

Do not be afraid to dream, always longing for the best
while leaving the unrest.

Do not be afraid to dream as you find your way in the storm,
seeking and searching for perfect form.

Do not be afraid to dream, abandon the content,
and search for the truth.

Do not be afraid to dream, look for the changing of the season,
in all of this there is a reason.

Do not be afraid to dream, the unborn wait the day,
their chosen direction expect your say.

Do not be afraid to dream, passion will give you hope,
endless love will help you cope.

"Never is there cold nor hurt and hearts know joy, while love is abundant."

Serenity

In the midst of the sparkling clear ocean the waves
come slowly towards the shore,
and there is serenity.

During the night the moon shines quietly on the sea
while radiance meets the dark, glory meets the light,
and there is serenity.

At night a shooting star graces the heavens,
and all eyes look to the beyond,
and there is serenity.

Never is there cold nor hurt and hearts know joy,
while love is abundant in everything,
and there is serenity.

Her soul is calling and searching,
longing for a sacred peace and meaning,
and there is serenity.

The glory is plentiful for us,
all of it good like the deep, true,
and there is serenity.

"There is a place at the table for you, holding your candle, keeping your light."

Well Into the Night

There is a place at the table for you,
holding your candle, keeping your light.
There is a place at the table for you,
where I have sat and watched you well into the night.

There is a place at the table for you,
where no one else will ever be able to sit.
There is a place at the table for you,
where only you could possibly fit.

There is a place across the table from you,
where a heart beats quickly with glow.
There inside is magic now,
and all of it ready to flow.

There is a place at the table for you,
holding your candle, keeping your light.
There is a place at the table for you,
where I have sat and watched you well into the night.

"There will be no more hurt for you, as the pain will be pushed aside."

Towards the Ground

Life will come together for you one dawning,
and all of the fallen leaves will dance towards the ground.

The willows will run with the wind,
and the clouds will drift across the sun-filled skies.

There will be no more hurt for you,
as the pain will be pushed aside.

What was once so unsightly will bloom wonderful and marvelous,
and all will want to see.

Begin again, begin again, be stronger and wiser,
and live as your spirit and your soul demands.

Life will come together for you one dawning,
and all of the fallen leaves will dance towards the ground.

"There is peace again
and the calm has replaced
the distress."

Spring Again

It is spring again, and all of the birds begin to fly.
It is spring again, and all of the flowers will never die.

It is spring again, and the sparrows bless the trees.
It is spring again, as the children come off their knees.

There is light again, as you have arrived and graced this place.
There is peace again, and the calm has replaced the race.

It is spring again, and I will be your friend
in the cold and the rain.

It is spring again,
as I touch your face and hold close your name.

Stay here forever, and enjoy the changing seasons.
You gave me flowers, I will give you reason.

It is spring again, and the hills turn when you pass.
It is spring again, time for love that will forever last.

"*I* have seen you on your knees, the cold freezing your heart."

Fallen and Kissed

I have seen you grow and watched your fears.
I have seen your smiles and traced your tears.

I have seen you at night, alone and amiss.
I have seen you fallen, weary and un-kissed.

I have seen you on your knees, the cold freezing your heart.
I have seen you laugh and watched you depart.

I have seen your courage, the forcefulness of your will.
I have seen you in triumph and in loss.

I have seen you in hunger, in thirst and pain.
I have seen you walk the yard in the rain.

I have looked into your eyes and seen the moon flow.
I have met your spirit, watched it spread, expand and grow.

"You will love the water and learn to praise the sea. You will find comfort in the breezes and strength in me."

Tortola Brown

There is an island blessed by the Caribbean sun that
is a splendid place for you and for me.
Tortola Brown

There are lovely beaches with sparkling warm sands
where young children play and souls know tender demands.
Tortola Brown

There is a young green hill where coconuts grow,
where lovers roam at night, to and fro.
Tortola Brown

There is an old fish market right before your eyes,
where your first child will be born, and cry.
Tortola Brown

You will love the water and learn to praise the sea,
you will find comfort in the breezes and strength in me.
Tortola Brown

"Please be my ally, my comforter and friend, I will help you in the winter until the spring comes in."

The Winter Came

You left me just before the winter came,
and the flowers fell lifeless, and I the same.

I needed you deeply before the solace broke,
unable to hear music nor see through the smoke.

My days are overflowing yet empty still,
there are things I must do, but have little will.

I want to hold you gently and whisper in your ear,
but you are away, not close, not here.

Yet you have been present during these nights,
you have been my darling, my constant delight.

Please be my ally, my comforter and friend,
I will help you in the winter until the spring comes in.

You left me just before the winter came,
and the flowers fell lifeless, and I the same.

"If all the children were fed each night and every moment was fair, would you dear love take hold their hands and show them that you care?"

Were But a Rose

If all of the winter were but a rose,
and chaos did not exist,
would you dear love turn your back
and pursue madness to its end?

If all the children were fed each night and every moment was fair,
would you dear love take hold their hands
and show them that you care?

If all the aged were comforted and bliss and never left alone,
would you dear love remember their names or deeds
when they passed on?

If all the world were but a rose, and you found yourself robust,
would there be room for others like you, for differences,
for sanity and trust?

If all the world were but a rose, and life seemed plain and true,
would you dear love be as you are, and love me as you do?

"You are troubled
and your heart is abound.
I understand and will go
for now."

I Understand

*M*any can be your lover,
but few will be your friend.

Some will warm your bed at night,
yet will not remain until the end.

Love comes and goes like mist in the air,
a fog sometimes, with depression and despair.

You are troubled and your heart is abound,
I understand and will go for now.

Love is like life, often up and often down,
and the silence cries while falling and rushes to the ground.

Sometimes we doubt the strength of the wind,
from the south it comes, a note from a friend.

It may be forever before you take your place,
go but take your time during this race.

You are troubled and your heart is abound.
I understand and will go for now.

"Remain just as lovely as I found you, for I will send you missives, bring you lace and build a home."

Thunder and Rise

If ever you should leave me,
the sun would cease to dance across the sky.
The earth would stop, and all that is good
would pass bye and bye.

For you have given new meaning to my living
and held my heart close to your eyes,
you have shown me the morning, the amber,
the thunder and the rise.

And often I sit to look upon you,
even when you are not near.
Sometimes I call out your name,
wishing that you were here.

Remain just as lovely as I found you,
for I will send you missives,
bring you lace and build a home.

Love me from this day forward
through the gentle and turbulent toss.
Press my heart to your bosom,
for without you I am surely lost.

"The midst of youth finds you sullen and worn, you chase illusions unable to survive the storm."

Not Surviving the Storm

In the coldest part of the world,
I stand between the ice and the windward bands.

Detached and lonely my heart cries foul, you fool,
you pushed her away, to the side.

So proud and daring to think that all you needed
was laughter and a pen.

And they have not carried you through these days
as your eyes stare at your work,
while your mind is many miles away.

The midst of youth finds you sullen and worn,
you chase illusions, unable to survive the storm.

You may lose her this morning,
you may well during the night.

Once the future held promise,
now all is displeasing, and little is bright.

"*I*ts sacred agent, solitude, presents an unfaithful abyss that is all-encompassing and knows little joy."

Loneliness

Loneliness is like the most horrifying of monsters,
approaching wickedly while we are weak.

Its sacred agent, solitude, presents an unfaithful abyss
that is all-encompassing and knows little joy.

During the height of the darkness, the solitary ponder
all loves once had in search of the most infinite of memories.

It is not unlike the worst of all tortures, the rising of the sun, too,
signals another sad day leading to its conclusion.

It is hopelessness and fatigue, and a spirit trapped
within margins defined by ominous walls.

"Between the pains and the hurt, remember—Love you I do."

Love You I Do

Between the darkness and the light, remember
Love you I do.

Between the yellows and the reds, remember
Love you I do.

Between the pain and the hurt, remember
Love you I do.

Between the laughter and the joy, remember
Love you I do.

Between the wicked and the evil, remember
Love you I do.

Between the mountains and the valleys, remember
Love you I do.

"This song has pierced my life and given me silver and gold."

This Song

This song you sing in the early hours,
at the noon and late at night.

This song brings movement and dancing,
cheerfulness and delight.

This song has touched a cord so deep it pains,
yet still my heart is safe, and I am sane.

This song makes me feel like a new child,
running through the windswept hills.

This song has fed me like a mother,
it keeps me and has made me another.

This song has pierced my life,
and given me silver and gold.

This song has been a vibrant joy,
and has chased the shadows of old.

"After the feast I slept. The morning brought the eastern sun, and I laughed."

My Ebony Rose

And somehow I just wanted you to know that I was afraid,
but your glow helped me,
My ebony rose.

I sensed that you knew and that you were frightened too,
yet never said so,
My ebony rose.

After the feast I slept. The morning brought the eastern sun,
and I laughed as a thousand rainbows danced before my eyes,
My ebony rose.

Perhaps it will not happen again. There will be no tears,
and you can maintain your guarded balance,
My ebony rose.

It is quiet now, and the once dark candle still burns as it did
that rather special night,
My ebony rose.

"Your truth is greater than all the truths, come by here."

Come By Here

*H*ere your dreams will find their sight,
come by here.

Here my heart will lay aside your fears,
come by here.

Your gifts are beyond what heroes give,
come by here.

Your truth is greater than all the truths,
come by here.

Once a star was set in the sky for you,
come by here.

And the world is better because of that view,
come by here.

The peace of the earth is yours,
come by here.

There is the promise of something new and good,
come by here.

"I stand here at this rim, cold and alone. In my heart beats a worrisome tone."

The Edge of the Earth

I walked to the edge of the earth,
I stood near the rim. I thought of our love
and all things grew dim.

That dashing feeling once in our souls
had grown weaker and lighter and suddenly old.

I once loved you beyond all reason.
Now all that is changed,
love is lost, gone, treason.

You were my queen and I your king,
and like in a dream all through,
now there is nothing.

I stand here at this rim, cold and alone.
In my heart beats a worrisome tone.

For me this love can be no more.
I have lost. We have lost. No more.

Now I will go, I know not where,
perhaps to find another love somewhere.

Here at this edge all is dim,
and my spirit tells me to leave this rim.

"There are children in your future, there is great peace in your heart. Now I know."

Now I Know

There is a rainbow in your eyes,
there is magic in your face.
Now I know.

There is glory in your soul,
there is sweetness in your grace.
Now I know.

There are children in your future,
there is great peace in your heart.
Now I know.

There is a mountain waiting for you to climb,
where flowers will never cease to grow.
Now I know.

And there each day you will be loved,
and revered, and sadly missed.
Now I know.

"Now all I have is thee,
the dew runs swiftly down my
spine."

When All I Had Was Me

When all I had was me, the burning pain would come,
like water ruining the rum, while my near gone soul did flee.

When all I had was me, the wheat seeds planted would not grow,
the sunlight I did seldom know.

When all I had was me, I walked home sadly each day,
the world but a tragic display,
an abundance of pain the decree.

When all I had was me, the sand ran slowly down the glass,
my fate cast with that of the last,
there was no turning key.

Now all I have is thee, the dew runs swiftly down my spine,
birds and flowers fill every line,
not for a moment again, me alone with me.

"The hour is sweet, and like a whisper, I cannot do this alone."

From Eternity to Eternity

I will love you now and even when the wind ceases
to carry the fragrances,
From Eternity to Eternity.

I will hold your hand and walk through the wilderness
to the fruits of the promised land,
From Eternity to Eternity.

While apart I did never forget you or your faithfulness,
From Eternity to Eternity.

The hour is sweet, and like a whisper,
I cannot do this alone and afraid,
From Eternity to Eternity.

In love there can be truth and peace,
life is blessed, and abundantly so,
From Eternity to Eternity.

"Come make love to me, celebrate this joy, this hope, this reign."

Make Love to Me

Come make love to me,
and hold my hand during the night.

Come make love to me,
let me touch you true and bright.

Come make love to me,
see the colors, the warmth, never the shame.

Come make love to me,
celebrate this joy, this hope, this reign.

Come make love to me,
before the winter snow covers the plains.

"The skies are dark, and the stars are hidden. Yet somewhere there is love, dear."

Somewhere There Is Love, Dear

The roses fade as the hours and days do pass.
The early frost comes, and it is cold and lonely.

The skies are dark, and the stars are hidden.
Yet somewhere there is love, dear.

It is all quiet as the earth refuses to speak.
The streams are dry, and the leaves fallen.

There is a storm in the air, the wind is brisk.
Yet somewhere there is love, dear.

Most are weary and worn, and sparkle has escaped.
There is little freshness and hope recedes.

At times it hurts to love.
Movement is slow, and the sad echo chants.
Yet somewhere there is love, dear.

"*I* saw you once while watching the moon at night. You spoke to me, telling me that all would be fine and that my dreams would come true."

Watching the Storm

I saw you once while watching the moon at night.
I was cold and alone, and you warmed me.

I saw you once while watching the moon at night.
And you wrote a tapestry of hope that settled my heart,
and made me whole.

I saw you once while watching the moon at night.
You spoke to me, telling me that all would be fine and
that my dreams would come true.

I saw you once while watching the moon at night.
You came to me, kissed my lips and led me home.

"*It* would be unfair to mark your soul when you have such a great and inspiring need."

One Day Soon

I am leaving because I cannot allow my heart to bleed,
one day soon.

It would be unfair to mark your soul
when you have such a great and inspiring need,
one day soon.

I wander from place to place,
I rest but I go on as I must,
one day soon.

The grays come together and they meet,
somewhere near the blues,
one day soon.

I try to hold them apart, but am unable,
I do not want to leave you,
one day soon.

"In search of a note I write you a letter and kiss it while mailing, and I find my music."

In Search of a Note

In search of a note I listen to the silence,
to bring me my music.

In search of a note I tend to the fools that I find around me,
to bring me my music.

In search of a note I hold the unknown,
to bring me my music.

In search of a note I run to the corner to chase a lost feather,
to bring me my music.

In search of a note I go to the mailbox to greet your brief missives,
and I find my music.

In search of a note I write you a letter and kiss it while mailing,
and I find my music.

In search of a note I watch the passing of the drifting blues,
and I find my music.

In search of a note I wake in the morning, my thoughts turn to you,
and I find my music.

"In the midst of the dawn
the early birds speak of reason
and all is refreshingly clear."

Dawn

In the midst of the dawn the lights draw near,
sounds capture the silence,
and the morning rays admonish needless fears.

In the midst of the dawn the skies grow blue,
and behind the clouds is a promise of something special,
something new.

In the midst of the dawn the frozen waters
drop from the leaves, as though they were children's tears.

And at last the morning glory opens its eyes,
all at once, fresh and green.

In the midst of the dawn the early birds speak of
reason, and all is refreshingly clear.

In the midst of the dawn the earth turns,
while people once trodden and untitled
know that the light is not too distant now.

"And I want to go forward to search and not to yield."

Stardust

On the tip of my heart,
at the center of my bow,
is a melody of lyrics
and stardust below.

And the light that it gives
brightens the world and its days,
like an assortment of lilies
chasing the confusion away.

I would have never known
if I had been weak and afraid,
but the stardust did shake me
and at its side I did lay.

And I want to go forward
to search and not to yield,
I want to understand you
and help us to build.

Like a panther in the wild,
like a blade in the grass,
my love grows daily,
there is meaning at last.

"Love's joy knows no sorrow, its pleasantries outweigh remorse."

Love's Depth

Love's depth knows no depth,
just as some leave few challenges undone.

Love's breath does not cease,
just as horizons never begin nor end.

Love's worth knows no worth,
even without riches it brings wealth.

Love's joy knows no sorrow,
its pleasantries outweigh remorse.

Love's peace knows no madness,
it brings kindness like that of simple times.

Love's strength knows no weakness,
it enables us to go forever forward.

Love's depth knows no depth,
just as some leave few challenges undone.

"Fill my cup until it runs over, let your rivers run wide inside of me."

Fill My Cup

In the middle of the night
before the dusk met the dawn,
I laid my soul next to you
and prayed that I could be reborn.

When the storm came that evening
and all seemed certain to end,
I reached out to your being
and held you as my only friend.

I wanted to be yours forever,
reaching sweetly for serenity,
loving you as best I could,
asking only that you love me.

Fill my cup until it runs over,
let your rivers run wide inside of me.
Come closer and closer to new life,
let me love, need and cherish thee.

My belief in you runs deep,
wings of the morning led me to you.
Never again will I face the river alone,
as long as I lay in your keep.

"Flood not the valley,
risking its loss one day.
Time tells all."

Time Tells All

If you need time, you have time.
If you need space, you have space.
Time tells all.

I have needed time to clear,
to breathe the freshness of the air.
Time tells all.

Rush not a jewel for it may slip away.
Flood not the valley, risking its loss one day.
Time tells all.

The blind man says wait,
be her friend in the market square.
Time tells all.

"*I* shall find the strength inside my soul, and only love you."

Only Love You

I shall place the past behind me now,
and only love you.

I shall leave the hurt outside the door,
and only love you.

I shall toss the memories of fallen times,
and only love you.

I shall find the strength inside my soul,
and only love you.

I shall give you my heart until my final day,
and only love you.

"Somewhere a star calls out your name. It sings that life will not be the same."

Somewhere

Somewhere a light shines for you, my dear,
and the light will forever glow far and near.

Somewhere a chariot waits for you, my lace,
simply call it, blessing it with your grace.

Somewhere a star calls out your name,
it sings that life will not be the same.

Somewhere a rose is planted for you neatly,
its sweetness is yours, with ease and completely.

"Did fate ever take you away, my sweet, my hands would tremble as I stare."

My Sweet

Will it that fate ever take you away, my sweet,
and leave me alone, cold with nothing
but walls and a dream shattered.

Dare fate ever take you away, my sweet,
my eyes would be dry no more,
my heart would send chills to my soul.

If fate did ever take you away, my sweet,
a shell I would become,
and beachmen would toss me to the sea.

Did fate ever take you away, my sweet,
my hands would tremble as I stare,
I would only sit and ponder why.

Yet if fate were never to take you, my sweet,
the joys that we would know,
the splendidness of our sleep.

The sanity we would bring,
the songs that we could sing,
the birth of a joyous spring.

"I would find for us a cabin where we could rest, where we could wander and play."

Wander and Play

I would bring you yellow roses to weave
into your life, and your hair.

If only I knew that you loved me too,
and for my heart you would care.

I would give you blue asters,
and gather sea shells from the shore.

If only I knew that you loved me too,
ensuring my love and giving me more.

I would find a cabin where we could spend each day,
where we could rest, wander and play.

Yet if you were not to love me or consider what I say,
I would sadly turn on love, and slowly walk away.

"The times we danced in between the rain drops, alone when love was never undone."

Odd This Way

All too well I know your heart aches,
as I did wrong your soul.

I brought you sleepless nights,
fraught with anger and unnecessary cold.

I made you sad. Your laugh no longer there,
I brought you winter, and none of it was fair.

But remember the gladness that we once had,
the warmth of the island sun.

The times we danced in between the rain drops,
alone when love was never undone.

And while that was so many years gone by,
so very distant they need not be.

Can you love me again until the ambers come,
when we can sing, dance, laugh and be.

"It has hurt so much you not being near, once the evenings brought joy, not this fear."

My Lady

Early one morning I reached for your light,
as things were uneven during a troubled night.

At first you seemed twisted, but then it was all very young,
you were brave, fresh, spirited and full of fun.

My heart took to you like the red leaves in the fall,
after a while it came back broken, all.

When you went to anchor I cast you away,
I tried forgetting while my soul was at bay.

It has hurt so much you not being near,
once the evenings brought joy, not this terrible fear.

My lady, I will wait through this night.
My lady, I will live so that we might.

"My love does not like to stand in the rain, but the pressing of her hand erases my pain."

Immensely Indeed

My love does not have much to say,
the rock of my love is her manner, her way.

My love does not close her eyes when we kiss,
and when the night comes she is often remiss.

My love does not always look my way,
yet the sparkle in her glow speaks of a new day.

My love does not like to stand in the rain,
but the pressing of her hand erases my pain.

My love does not sit by the water to read,
yet I love my love immensely, immensely indeed.

"For your love belongs to the world, not simply to one as undeserving as me."

Walk Softly

Walk softly during this night, my love,
the storm is finished and the flowers are watered.

Your bare pounding breasts press closely,
and I feel you and see fields of plenty.

I have waited for your love all of my life,
yet I am tempted like a fearful deer to run.

For your love belongs to the world,
not simply to someone as undeserving as me.

While with you I am as the prophets were,
blessedly whole, strong and resolute.

Without you I am frightened and chilled,
like a small child on a December day.

I have loved you not beyond reason, but
within reason, and with my fullest love.

Walk softly during this night, my love,
the storm is finished and the flowers are watered.

"*I* once loved you, dear ocean, reaching often for you with delight."

Dear Ocean

I once loved you, dear ocean,
your mighty waves and magnificent roar.

I once loved you, dear ocean,
your greens bleeding, your blues true.

I once loved you, dear ocean,
watching and waiting and listening for more.

I once loved you, dear ocean,
reaching often for you with delight.

Now suddenly I loathe you, dear ocean,
you have taken her away from me.

And it has not been the same, dear ocean,
I am alone, less than sane and free.

Little did I know, dear ocean,
that you would abscond with my love.

Now I abhor thee, dear ocean,
the sun rises on a distant shore, and I mourn.

Yet I could still love thee, dear ocean,
please let me stand blissful, release these thorns.

"Thank you for stopping me from the silly roles. Thank you for erasing the pain from my soul."

Thank You

Thank you for loving me while I was most alone.
Thank you for chatting with me endlessly on the phone.

Thank you for kissing my sweat-covered brow.
Thank you for drying my eyes and telling me how.

Thank you for being different from the weak.
Thank you for truth and for challenging the meek.

Thank you for coming with me out into the cold.
Thank you for giving me vigor when I was not bold.

Thank you for stopping me from the silly roles.
Thank you for erasing the pain from my soul.

Thank you for the tulips that Sunday noon.
Thank you for roses, the hope and the moon.

"Grab hold my soul and be my princess, and allow me to be your prince."

Grab Hold My Soul

Grab hold my soul and go with me to where
the horizon meets the fleeting seas.

Grab hold my soul and never lose me
nor cease loving me, or being my friend.

Grab hold my soul and hold my hand,
until tomorrow embraces tomorrow.

Grab hold my soul and leave the pain,
for I will love you beyond the mountains.

Grab hold my soul and run with me,
as my world needs you so badly.

Grab hold my soul and be my princess,
and allow me to be your prince.

Grab hold my soul and fill this void,
never again will you know the darkness deep.

Grab hold my soul and light my life,
pushing away misery and strife.

"Now I am forever the better, not at the end again, only the start."

Flowers and Lace

I have watched you sing in autumn,
I have watched you crossing the stage.
I have looked into your blazing fire
and each time I am amazed.

It is much more than your style,
that intrigues me from day to day.
It is a part of your soul
that keeps me from running away.

Perhaps I will never know,
what makes you who you are.
Our paths may never cross again.
You may stay here, and I go afar.

But you I will always keep,
for you have touched my heart.
Now I am forever the better,
not at the end again, only the start.

You shine like a star in the twilight,
watching the world while it moves.
And as you go forward in life,
you will win and never lose.

"Know that I know you have been unloved, and that you expect the coming of treason."

There Is Warmth Here

Like the first Christmas this joy is true.
It rains outside, but there is warmth here.

The morning sun speaks of glory,
and there is character in your eyes.

The depth of my conscience says forward,
grab hold this comet and burning light.

Set your own pace while the twisted watch,
it is not important to be among the first.

Know that I know you have been unloved,
and that you expect the coming of treason.

I do not ask that you change your soul,
as I offer my own completely.

Just as the ocean turns to expunge the weed
you, my precious, will have rested your need.

Like the first Christmas this joy is true.
It rains outside, but there is warmth here.

"The world has known you forever, as you are a part of its spirit that is good and bold."

You Bring Hope

And like the night before the coming year,
you hold promise of something new.

Not unlike a fresh star riding the sky,
lighting the heavens and cleansing the deep.

Life is difficult, yet you continue on,
like a shepherd walking among her flock.

The world has known you forever, as you
are a part of its spirit that is good and bold.

More than a thousand times you've cried,
as the burdens trespassed, but you have won.

It is written that you would come,
with something of value and of rarity.

Listen to the quiet as you dash through the valley,
there is sweet music playing for you.

Soon the magic will fill your heart,
dance for you are the angel of hope.

"*Each* morning after we have slept, I will give you lilacs, fresh berries and tell you tales of sweet romance."

Each Morning

Each morning when the sun begins its rise,
joy will be your solitude and I will remove
the sleep from your eyes.

Each morning after we have slept,
I will give you lilacs, fresh berries
and tell you tales of sweet romance.

Each morning after the angels sing,
the sparrows will take flight and comfort
the trade winds will bring.

Each morning after the tears and the dreams,
the light will come and the earth will rejoice,
and all will be good.

Each morning when the rainbows grace the skies,
the melons will ripen while the sweetness of
daylight will be your surprise.

Each morning after your sea bath and your
glance at the dove, you will be happy and thrilled
and rejoice in abundant love.

"Hurt, but when she pained I closed my eyes, and refused to hear her suffering."

Such a Fool

Such a fool when all that she offered was love,
and there I stood stoically
with my eyes fixed only on the moment.

Now at the bottom, pursuing her love like a gambler
desperate for a fortune.

Longing for her touch and seeing her face in the night.

The spring has once again come,
yet the winter maintains its grip.
The cold is bitter and rude.

Hurt, but when she pained I closed my eyes,
and refused to hear her suffering.

In time all are called, and now my name has been spoken,
and I must answer.

Such a fool when all that she offered was love,
and there I stood stoically
with my eyes fixed only on the moment.

www.ingramcontent.com/pod-product-compliance
Lightning Source LLC
LaVergne TN
LVHW022318080426
835509LV00036B/2591